S0-BMR-685

# CHARITIES IN ACTION

## CARING FOR ANIMALS

*Liz Gogerly*

*Chicago, Illinois*

**www.capstonepub.com**
Visit our website to find out more information about Heinemann-Raintree books.

**To order:**
☎ Phone 800-747-4992
🖥 Visit www.capstonepub.com to browse our catalog and order online.

© 2012 Heinemann Library
an imprint of Capstone Global Library, LLC
Chicago, Illinois

All rights reserved. No part of this publication may be reproduced or transmitted in any form or by any means, electronic or mechanical, including photocopying, recording, taping, or any information storage and retrieval system, without permission in writing from the publisher.

Edited by Andrew Farrow, Adam Miller, and
 Diyan Leake
Designed by Victoria Allen
Picture research by Ruth Blair
Illustrations by Oxford Designers & Illustrators
Production by Victoria Fitzgerald

Originated by Capstone Global Library Ltd
Printed and bound in China by Leo Paper
 Products Ltd

16 15 14 13 12
10 9 8 7 6 5 4 3 2 1

**Library of Congress Cataloging-in-Publication Data**
Gogerly, Liz.
 Caring for animals / Liz Gogerly.—1st ed.
  p. cm.—(Charities in action)
 Includes bibliographical references and index.
 ISBN 978-1-4329-6384-2 (hb)—ISBN 978-1-4329-6391-0 (pb) 1. Animal welfare. 2. Voluntarism. 3. Animal shelters. I. Title.
 HV4708.G564 2013
 636.08'32—dc23          2012000580

**Acknowledgments**
The author and publisher are grateful to the following for permission to reproduce copyright material: Alamy pp. 5 (© Peter Horree), 29 (© Marc Hill), 41 (© AF archive), 47 (© Mike Hughes Photography); Corbis pp. 13 (© A. Inden), 39 (© Specialist Stock), 57 (© Julie Dermansky); © The Donkey Sanctuary p. 49; Getty Images pp. 31 (Mario Tama), 45 (Frederick M. Brown), 53 (Rob Elliott/AFP); © George Logan pp. 6, 8; North Downs Picture Agency © Roger Allen pp. 20, 22; PA Photos p. 50 (Ben Birchall); Photoshot p. 25 (© Imagebrokers); Reuters p. 33 (Kim Kyung-Hoon ); Shutterstock pp. 15 (© palko72), 18 (© Yvonne Pijnenburg-Schonewille), 17 (© Hung Chung Chih), 34 (© Alvaro Pantoja), 37 (© Willyam Bradberry), 40 (© Bill Mathies), 43 (© FloridaStock), 55 (© Germanskydiver).

Cover photograph of Debbie Cox of the Jane Goodall Institute working with protected chimpanzees reproduced with permission of Corbis (© Penny Tweedie).

Every effort has been made to contact copyright holders of material reproduced in this book. Any omissions will be rectified in subsequent printings if notice is given to the publisher.

**Disclaimer**
All the Internet addresses (URLs) given in this book were valid at the time of going to press. However, due to the dynamic nature of the Internet, some addresses may have changed, or sites may have changed or ceased to exist since publication. While the author and publisher regret any inconvenience this may cause readers, no responsibility for any such changes can be accepted by either the author or the publisher.

# CONTENTS

Words printed in **bold** are explained in the glossary.

# WHO CARES FOR ANIMALS?

All around the world, there are charities in action that protect and care for animals. Teams of dedicated employees and volunteers work together for the **welfare** of all kinds of animals. Some people work directly with animals, but there are also professionals behind the scenes, in laboratories and in marketing, **publicity**, finance, and fund-raising departments—all doing their part to help the animals.

Members of the public volunteer their time, too. Local charities rely upon volunteers to give hands-on help, such as cleaning out cages or walking dogs. In addition, national charities need fund-raisers and the public to back their **campaigns** to protect the future of **endangered species**.

## Born Free

The story of the Born Free Foundation is an example of how people can do mighty things when they are touched by the plight of animals. The actress Virginia McKenna and her husband, Bill Travers, starred together in the movie *Born Free* in 1966. The movie was based on the true story of George and Joy Adamson's attempts to release a lioness named Elsa into the wilds of Kenya, in East Africa. Virginia and Bill were moved by the story, and they were inspired to help other wild animals living in **captivity** get released back to the wild.

## The lonely elephant

Bill began by making wildlife **documentaries**. Next, the couple campaigned to free Pole Pole, a young female elephant that had been captured and taken from her family in Africa to England's London Zoo, where she lived without any other elephants. Distressed and lonely, Pole Pole died when she was just 16. (Elephants often live to be about 60.)

Pole Pole's sad existence inspired Virginia and Bill. Together with their son, Will Travers, they set up the charity Zoo Check in 1984. Their aim was to save animals from a life of captivity and to phase out zoos worldwide. The Born Free Foundation evolved from Zoo Check to become one of the most proactive and respected animal welfare charities in the world.

## Born Free today

Today, the Born Free Foundation helps and campaigns to protect big cats, elephants, **primates**, and **marine life**. It has helped all kinds of creatures, from baboons and basking sharks to orca and orangutans. Sometimes Born Free responds to the urgent needs of an individual creature and finds it a place of **sanctuary**. Other times, the organization campaigns against the exploitation of animals, such as hunting or illegal trading.

Most animal charities need your help. Dog walking is a rewarding way of volunteering your time. This man helps out at his local dog rescue center in Argentina.

## What is a charity?

A charity, or charitable organization, is a type of voluntary organization that reaches out to help those in need. To be declared a registered charity, the organization must be independent of the government, not-for-profit, and of benefit to the public. Charities have to be managed and run their finances according to a number of rules, which vary by state.

# The story of Dolo the lion

Sometimes the rescue of one animal can take years of planning and perseverance on the part of a whole team of charity workers and volunteers.

The story of Dolo the lion first caught many people's interest in 2006. A tourist in Dolo Odo village, in southern Ethiopia, was shocked to find an adult male lion chained inside a house. The four-year-old animal had been kept as an illegal pet since he was a cub. The 3-foot (1-meter) chain around his neck was so tight that it dug into his flesh. The subdued animal could hardly walk because he had been chained for so long. The tourist took a photograph of the sad creature. Soon afterward, the Born Free Foundation and other animal welfare groups began campaigning for his release.

## Emergency action!

In 2007, the Ethiopian Wildlife Conservation Authority, with the help of the Born Free Foundation, organized the rescue of Dolo. The rescue team included a veterinarian, a vet's assistant, drivers, armed scouts, and a government official with the paperwork required for **confiscating** the animal.

John Knight, a vet working with Born Free, is shown here with Dolo the lion. The vet **sedates** and examines Dolo before he is relocated.

## Rescue mission

It was no easy mission. Upon the rescue team's arrival at Dolo Odo, 300 villagers protested against their lion being taken away. The Wildlife Authority explained that it is illegal in Ethiopia for wild animals to be kept in inadequate conditions and without a **permit**.
The team worked through the night. Shocked by how weak and sick the lion appeared, the vet worked quickly to **tranquilize** him.

Eventually, the chain around Dolo's neck was cut, and he was bundled into a cage that could be transported. It was too dangerous to stay in the village, so the team made a getaway. Driving through the night, they feared for the lion's life. When he awoke, he was sick and would not eat or drink.

Four days later, the rescue team arrived at Ethiopia's Awash National Park. Everyone was exhausted, but they were relieved that Dolo had survived the ordeal. When he was finally released into a bigger cage, he tried to walk. At first, he could hardly manage it, but soon he was savoring his first steps without being chained. This was just the beginning of Dolo's amazing story.

### Do your part

Like all animal welfare charities, the Born Free Foundation relies upon donations (gifts of money) from the public. It also encourages people to get involved by planning their own fund-raising events. Born Free distributes information packets filled with great ideas for fund-raising at school. Events like a car wash or holding a school dance or fashion show are just a few interesting suggestions.

### Keeping the numbers down

Born Free operates a nonbreeding policy for rescued animals. This means that any animals they rescue do not have babies. The charity adopts this policy to ensure the best use of limited sanctuary space.

## A place of sanctuary

Dolo's first years after the chain was removed were spent at the Awash National Park. Meanwhile, the Born Free Foundation, in partnership with the Ethiopian Wildlife Conservation Authority, was building Ensessakotteh, a new wildlife rescue center near the capital, Addis Ababa. In 2011, Dolo was relocated to his own new **enclosure** at the center. The planners and construction team had worked hard to make Dolo's new home as natural and "wild" as possible. There are trees and bushes for shade and plenty of grass for him to walk around. Dolo also has an indoor shelter and everything he needs to keep him safe from harm for the rest of his life. He has settled well in his new home and is even sharing his enclosure with a rescued lioness named Safia.

### Roar of contentment

"Today, [Dolo's] roar sounds out across Ensessakotteh, and he has space, grass under foot, peace, and privacy. He now looks magnificent and has regained some of the dignity that nature bestowed on him but humankind so cruelly robbed him of."

Stephen Brend, project director, BF Ethiopia

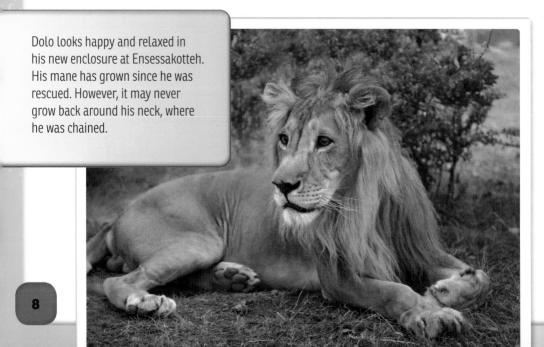

Dolo looks happy and relaxed in his new enclosure at Ensessakotteh. His mane has grown since he was rescued. However, it may never grow back around his neck, where he was chained.

## International charities

The story of Dolo the lion is uplifting. Although it is extraordinary, it is just one of many examples of how charities around the world are working hard to change the lives of endangered, sick, and rescued animals for the better.

Organizations such as WWF work around the globe. The WWF network has national branches in more than 100 countries. The national branches all share the same aims—primarily to protect the planet's natural environment and endangered species. National branches also campaign for the animals in their own country. For instance, WWF–New Zealand campaigns and protects the future of its endangered Hector's dolphins. In addition to large organizations like WWF, there are also many smaller global charities, such as the World Parrot Trust.

### Standing up for big cats

Big Cat Rescue (BCR) is a nonprofit educational sanctuary based in North Tampa, Florida. The sanctuary is home to more than 100 rescued big cats. The team at BCR suggest becoming an "AdvoCat." Anyone can sign up and receive regular bulletins about the latest laws affecting wild cats. They can then do their part by supporting or opposing these laws, depending on how they affect the animals.

## National charities

Most countries have their own national animal welfare charities. In the United States, the **Humane** Society is a very important national animal welfare organization. Independent Humane Society branches exist in most states. Another major organization is the American Society for the Prevention of Cruelty to Animals (ASPCA). Its mission is "to provide effective means for the prevention of cruelty to animals throughout the United States." Additionally, there are independent, local Society for the Prevention of Cruelty to Animals (SPCA) organizations.

Other important national charities around the world include the Royal Society for the Prevention of Cruelty to Animals (RSPCA) in England and Wales, the Société Protectrice des Animaux in France, and the Visakha Society for the Prevention of Cruelty to Animals in India. These charities have a network of local branches in towns and cities.

# World map of animal charities

Charities care for all kinds of animals all over the world. Small, local charities or nonprofit organizations are found in all countries. The map on page 11 locates the organizations mentioned in this book. It also highlights some of the areas where charities are helping animals in need.

## World Animal Day

World Animal Day (WAD) is on October 4 each year. It was founded in 1931 by a group of **ecologists** eager to help endangered species. As part of WAD, Party for Animals Worldwide (PAW) raises funds for animal charities through live music events. On WAD 2007, the singer Pink helped to raise over $88,000 for organizations including the Monkey Sanctuary Trust and Animals Asia Foundation. "I'm very happy giving my time to this worthwhile cause," said Pink. "I'm passionate about animal conservation across the world and through my involvement with PAW I believe we can greatly help raise awareness and funds for animal conservation and welfare charities worldwide."

## How charities use donations

All animal charities try to ensure that the money they receive is used as productively as possible. Each charity divides the donations in the way that works best for it. WWF uses 71 percent of its donations directly on conservation programs and field projects, campaigns, education, and raising awareness of the threats to the environment. Another 28 percent is used for fund-raising—which includes work such as advertising and staying in touch with existing supporters. WWF claims to make $4.50 for every $1.50 invested in fund-raising, so this is money well spent! The final 1 percent helps to cover legal and accounting costs.

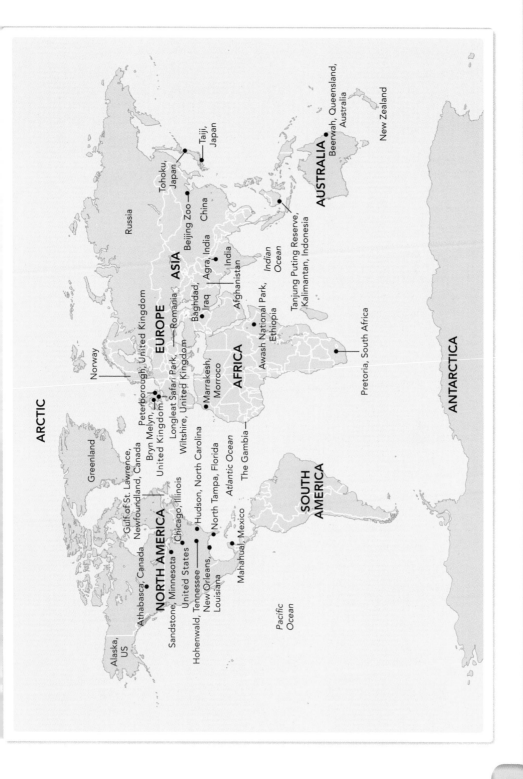

ARCTIC

NORTH AMERICA

Alaska, US

Greenland

Athabasca, Canada

Gulf of St. Lawrence, Newfoundland, Canada

Sandstone, Minnesota United States

Bryn Melyn, United Kingdom

Chicago, Illinois

Hohenwald, Tennessee

Hudson, North Carolina

New Orleans, Louisiana

North Tampa, Florida

Atlantic Ocean

The Gambia

Mahahual, Mexico

Pacific Ocean

SOUTH AMERICA

Norway

Peterborough, United Kingdom

EUROPE

Longleat Safari Park, Wiltshire, United Kingdom

Russia

Tohoku, Japan

Taiji, Japan

Beijing Zoo

China

Romania

ASIA

Baghdad, Iraq

Agra, India

India

Afghanistan

Marrakesh, Morroco

AFRICA

Awash National Park, Ethiopia

Tanjung Puting Reserve, Kalimantan, Indonesia

Indian Ocean

Pretoria, South Africa

AUSTRALIA

Beerwah, Queensland, Australia

New Zealand

ANTARCTICA

## Local charities

There are also many small, local charities helping animals in their area. These charities may be set up to run shelters, sanctuaries, or pet hospitals. They help all kinds of animals—from rescued cats, dogs, and other pets to local wildlife, such as injured badgers or captured kangaroos. For example, the Save the Manatee Club in Florida helps care for and rescue sick and injured manatees. The Hacienda de los Milagros in Chino Valley, Arizona, provides sanctuary for mules, donkeys, ponies, and horses. They all work toward the same goal of helping animals in need—and educating people in the process.

### Baghdad Pups

The Operation Baghdad Pups program was started by SPCA International. This charity brings the dogs rescued by servicemen and women in Afghanistan and Iraq back to the United States. On September 11, 2007, SPCA International received an e-mail from a U.S. soldier that moved them to take action. Sergeant Edward Watson was serving in Baghdad, Iraq. During his stay, his regiment had rescued a starving, flea-bitten puppy. The soldiers named it Charlie. The regiment was near the end of its deployment and wanted to bring Charlie back to the United States. However, soldiers are not supposed to befriend or bring back animals from a war zone using military transportation. Luckily, the story had a happy ending for Charlie. Members of the SPCA International team flew to Baghdad to rescue him, and he now lives with Sergeant Watson in Arizona. More than 300 other dogs and cats adopted by troops in the Middle East have also been rescued and brought back to the United States.

Many teenagers can volunteer to help charities that support and care for animals. Volunteers may be asked to feed the animals or clean out their living quarters.

## Helping people to care for animals

All around the world, people struggle to care for their animals as well as their families. Sometimes it is easy to forget that this can be the case in **developed countries** as well as poor countries. In the United States, charities such as Angels 4 Animals and the Pet Fund help the sick and injured animals of poor people. These groups work with veterinarians to provide affordable or free veterinary care for people who cannot afford to pay for a vet.

### Free services

In Illinois, the Anti-Cruelty Society has been helping pet owners since 1899. It also offers **neutering**, **vaccinations**, and **microchipping** of pets at a reduced cost. Also in the United States, the Found Animals Foundation holds a "SpayinLA" Day. Over a weekend, the organization offers up to 450 free **spays** or neutering operations for dogs and cats owned by low-income residents of Los Angeles. The charity believes that spaying and neutering pets is important work that has long-term benefits for animals, owners, and the community.

# MAKING A WORLD OF DIFFERENCE

The welfare of animals and the protection of endangered species is at the heart of the work of all international animal charities. Organizations such as Polar Bears International help just one species, while others campaign to help all kinds of animals.

## WWF

WWF is the world's largest independent conservation charity, with nearly 5 million members globally. Initially, the charity was set up to protect endangered species such as the giant panda. The organization launched in 1961 in Switzerland. That year, Chi Chi the giant panda was moved from Beijing Zoo to London Zoo and formed the inspiration for the charity's distinctive logo.

In the 21st century, the organization's mission is the conservation of nature, which means taking care of wildlife and wild places. Its goal is to reverse damage caused by humans to the environment and build a future in which humans live in harmony with nature. The organization strives to conserve plants and animals, including endangered species. This is a huge undertaking for any organization, but with a network of more than 100 national offices, the work of WWF makes a world of difference.

### How WWF raises money

Like all charities, WWF needs money to undertake its work. In 2010, WWF raised over $83 million from its members and donations from the public. Members can help by "adopting" endangered animals, donating cash, and by getting involved in fund-raising events. By adopting any symbolic animal, such as the panda, polar bear, or Emperor penguin, a person is supporting WWF's worldwide conservation efforts. There are more than 100 species to adopt, but the tiger is the most popular choice. It is one of the most threatened species—it is believed there are only about 3,200 tigers left in the wild. WWF aims to double the wild tiger population in the world by 2022, which happens to be the next Chinese Year of the Tiger. It hopes to do this by protecting the key places where the tiger has the best opportunity to thrive.

The Bengal tiger is the national animal of India and Bangladesh. Even so, humans are the biggest threat to these mighty beasts. The illegal trade of skins and body parts between India, Nepal, and China contributes to its decline in numbers.

### Leonardo DiCaprio

Hollywood actor Leonardo DiCaprio is passionate about conservation efforts to save the tiger. In 2010, he donated $1 million to WWF's Save Tigers Now campaign. He also toured tiger habitats in Nepal and Bhutan with WWF to boost publicity for the campaign. Being a famous face certainly helps to publicize the work of WWF.

### People power

We all have the power to help animals. Whether you make a small donation, adopt an animal, become involved in a campaign, or simply do your part to reduce waste and pollution, you are helping to conserve the future for many different species.

### A face we trust: David Attenborough

Another famous face who backs the work of WWF is the **naturalist** David Attenborough, known for his television programs about nature. He has spent more than 50 years making wildlife documentaries. In 2011, the International Broadcasting Convention awarded him its highest award, the International Honor for Excellence, in recognition of his career in television and natural history. Among his best-known works are the *Wildlife on One* and *Life* series, which focus on all the major groups of animals and plants. In recent years, he has explored environmental issues in programs including *State of the Planet* (2000) and *The Truth About Climate Change* (2006). In *State of the Planet*, he asked us all to face up to our responsibilities, saying:

"The future of life on Earth depends on our ability to take action. Many individuals are doing what they can, but real success can only come if there's a change in our societies and our economics and in our politics. I've been lucky in my lifetime to see some of the greatest spectacles that the natural world has to offer. Surely we have a responsibility to leave for future generations a planet that is healthy, inhabitable by all species."

## Taking action for polar bears

The polar bear is another creature that is considered at risk of **extinction**. Its **natural habitat** is the ice-covered waters of the Arctic in Greenland, Svalbard (in Norway), northern Canada, Alaska, and Russia. **Global warming** and **climate change** are seriously affecting the Arctic region. The polar ice cap is melting earlier each year. Polar bears hunt on the sea ice during spring and early summer. With the ice disappearing earlier each year, they have less hunting time and therefore face the threat of starvation in the winter months. WWF works at many levels to help polar bears. Part of its work involves tackling climate change and other human threats to the Arctic environment, such as industry. It employs hundreds of scientists and researchers to record what is going on in the Arctic region and its impact upon nature.

### In the field with the polar bears

WWF also employs experts who work directly with polar bears, monitoring individual animals' health and movements within the region. WWF International Arctic Program Polar Bear Conservation Coordinator Geoff York has been working with polar bears in the WWF Alaska field office since the early 1990s. He spends two months each year, in the spring and fall, on the ice. During this time, he works directly with the polar bears, studying their behavior and checking their health.

Typically, Geoff's work involves sedating the bears with a dart gun. While a bear is sedated, he measures its weight and length. He takes samples of blood, hair, fat, and feces. Each animal is marked with paint so that the team can monitor births, illnesses, and deaths within the family groups. It is this kind of work that allows WWF to assess the state of the polar bear population and plan ways to protect the animal in the future.

The endangered giant panda is on the logo for the conservation group WWF. It is estimated that there are around 1,600 to 3,000 pandas living in the wild in China.

## Research and education

Polar Bears International is another charity working hard on behalf of the polar bear. This organization promotes conservation through research and education. It supports the work of leading scientists and other professionals working with polar bears. Research is undertaken on wild bears living in the Arctic. There are also studies of bears living in zoos, since some studies are impossible to conduct on wild animals.

Information about the polar bear is important because it increases people's understanding of how they live. This means that the charity can act in an informed way to protect the species during this critical time in its struggle for survival. Another important role of Polar Bears International is to inform governments and the general public about the scientific studies.

A polar bear prepares to jump between ice floes. Polar bears live and hunt on ice. Some experts believe that polar bears will disappear from the Arctic by 2050.

### Working together

*Like many other animal charities, Polar Bears International works together with other conservation and environmental charities. These groups have the same goal—to protect the environment and make the world a better place for animals and humans.*

## International Animal Rescue

International Animal Rescue (IAR) protects wild and domestic animals from suffering in all parts of the world. IAR offices in the United States, the Netherlands, and the United Kingdom deal with administration, publicity, and fund-raising. Hot spots for IAR include India, Indonesia, and Malta.

- *India*: IAR runs two veterinary clinics and rescue centers, and it funds two sanctuaries for rescued dancing bears.

- *Java, Indonesia*: IAR has a center for macaques and slow lorises.

- *Malta*: IAR runs its own bird **rehabilitation** hospital.

## Swinging into action for orangutans

IAR is also protecting orangutans. The orangutan is an endangered species. This Asian great ape is found only in the rain forests on the Indonesian islands of Borneo and Sumatra. Scientists believe that the total wild population of animals has decreased dramatically in recent years. Humans are mostly responsible for their decline. Some animals are hunted for food, while baby animals are sold as pets. Meanwhile, the rain forest—the apes' natural habitat—is disappearing at a rate of two football fields every minute because of logging, mining, and forest fires, and to make way for new palm-oil plantations.

### The Sumatran Orangutan Society (SOS)

*SOS also helps to care for orangutans. It focuses on protecting the forest and educating the local people about the animals and their habitat. SOS representatives visit schools to talk to the children about growing trees for wood, so that they do not need to cut down trees in the forest.*

## Orangutan Emergency Center

Destruction of the rain forest in Kalimantan, on the island of Borneo, poses a serious threat to orangutans. Until the IAR stepped in, there were no adequate facilities in the area for rescued orangutans. In 2009, IAR started planning a new rescue and rehabilitation center at Ketapang. Meanwhile, it installed a team of vets at a temporary center. By January 2010, the Ketapang center was caring for 12 orangutans. With medical attention, nutritious diets, and new enclosures, these animals were thriving. The long-term goal of the IAR is to release some of the orangutans back into protected areas of the rain forest. In the meantime, work on the brand-new emergency center goes on.

Mely the orangutan is brought to her new enclosure at Ketapang. When IAR came to her rescue, her arms were so weak she could not use them to climb.

### Diary of events

Working with the orangutans is rewarding, but it takes dedication and hard work. Nobody knows this better than the team of veterinarians, headed by veterinary director Karmele Llano Sanchez. The vets, including volunteer vets, report what happens at the center on the IAR web site and write about the animals in regular blogs. These blogs give some insight into the time and attention each animal receives. For example, each new arrival at the center is given a name and a thorough health exam while sedated.

## Yola's story

Many of the orangutans have had a difficult time in the rain forest. Yola, a young orangutan, was discovered near a part of the forest that had been cleared for a new palm-oil plantation. IAR believes that plantation workers killed and ate Yola's mother. When Yola arrived at the IAR temporary center in December 2009, she was stressed and aggressive toward other animals. At first, she was given her own enclosure. When the new center was completed, Yola was moved to a bigger enclosure and began playing with the other orangutans, through the bars to the next enclosure. In time, it is hoped that Yola can be released back into the wild.

## Monti's story

Monti was one of the first infants to be rescued and taken to the center in February 2010. This young female was about five months old when IAR received a tip that there was an orphaned infant being kept illegally in the Ketapang area. She was discovered at the home of a local family, who claimed they had found Monti alone in the jungle. IAR workers believe the truth was somewhat different. They think that the locals killed Monti's mother so that her baby could be sold as a pet.

## Caring for Monti

When Monti arrived at the center, she was small and needed lots of care from the vets. Like a human baby, she spent lots of time sleeping and drinking milk. By May 2010, the vets reported that Monti was eating bananas and climbing well in the enclosure she shared with other infant orangutans. They also noted the youngster's confidence and "strong personality."

These days, Monti shares the enclosure the vets have nicknamed "baby school" with other rescued infants. The new play area has plenty of playthings to keep the infants amused, including ropes, ladders, hammocks, barrels, and tires for swinging. Monti loves to climb and looks set for a future back in the rain forest.

## Forced to be a pet

Mely, a female orangutan, has a heart-wrenching story. Mely had been chained up and kept as a pet for 15 years when she was rescued in October 2010. She has found sanctuary at the center, but after so many years as a pet, she does not have the skills to feed and fend for herself. Also, she has not lived with other orangutans since she was a baby. The vets are not sure if she will be able to live in the wild again.

After a few months at the center at Ketapang, Mely gained weight. When she is not playing, she is asleep in her hammock.

## Supporting people who depend on animals

Sometimes the best way that charities can help animals is by supporting and educating the people who depend on animals in their everyday lives. People living in poor communities in Africa, Asia, the Middle East, and Central and South America often rely upon working animals such as horses, donkeys, mules, goats, and camels. When an animal is sick or injured, the family it supports may struggle to survive.

## SPANA

The Society for the Protection of Animals Abroad (SPANA) was founded in 1923 to improve the lives of working animals and to help raise people's awareness of animal welfare. It believes that helping people to care for animals improves the quality of life for animals and their owners. SPANA is active all over the world, including in Africa, China, Iraq, and Mongolia. In Morocco, SPANA has 10 veterinary centers, some of which are also used as education centers.

### Horse power

Tourists visiting the Moroccan city of Marrakesh often take a ride on carriages pulled by calèche horses. The owners rely on the horses for their livelihoods, so it is important that they stay healthy. SPANA has set up a health system for the horses. Each horse is marked and registered with the charity. Every six months, each animal is given a health exam. If the horse is unwell, the charity can stop the animal from working until it receives medical attention. Another simple but effective initiative is providing water troughs. Thanks to SPANA, the calèche horses have fresh water to drink along all the major routes through the city.

## Volunteer vets

The Gambia Horse and Donkey Trust is another charity supporting people and their working animals. It provides free veterinary support and advice to families and farmers living in the Gambia, one of Africa's poorest countries. It runs mobile clinics and has a hospital with stables for up to 25 horses and donkeys. One of its most exciting initiatives is the Donkey Club, in which young boys can learn to bond with and care for their animals. The organization is also involved with community development projects to boost the local economy. The trust relies upon a team of dedicated volunteer vets who come to Africa and offer their skills for free.

## Vet in action

"Life as a volunteer at Gambia Horse and Donkey Trust is not for the faint hearted," claimed one of the volunteer vets who worked in the Gambia. Joanna Melluish, who recently graduated from veterinary school, could not agree more! She set off to the Gambia for a month soon after graduation.

During Joanna's time as a volunteer, she helped to train local people about caring for the animals and contributed to a study about an infection that is seriously affecting animals living in the area. Three days a week, she visited the local *lumos* (markets), treating working horses and donkeys brought along by their owners. This is hard work in the best of conditions, but working in 104 degrees Fahrenheit (40 degrees Celsius) heat, with people who did not speak English, was a real challenge. The animals had various problems, from harness sores, leg injuries, wounds caused by beating or ill-fitting harnesses to severe cases of worms and serious tropical diseases.

One night, there were three emergency situations. First, Joanna treated a donkey with a fractured limb. Next, she performed a fetotomy (the removal of a dead fetus) on a donkey, with only a flashlight for light. Finally, she dressed the wounds of a badly burned donkey. Getting the bandages to stay on proved tricky. She said: "In the end, we got out our sewing kits and made him a pair of what could only be called donkey pants to hold the bandages in place!"

### Vet and teacher, too

During her stay, Joanna taught classes to the Gambian staff. Many of the team members were experienced in practical matters, but Joanna was able to teach them how to carry out a clinical examination on a horse and give them information about various drugs.

## Tough lessons

Joanna's time in the Gambia taught her some tough lessons. She discovered new things about herself, such as her ability to cope in an emergency situation without the facilities she took for granted at home. It was an experience she will never forget. She said: "The people we met during our time in the Gambia were extremely welcoming and very grateful for the work done by the charity. I feel very privileged to have been let into this community—if only for a short period of time—and to have been able to do a little to help them in their mission to improve the lives of the people and animals in this area."

The machines used in modern farming have not reached many parts of the world. These poor South African farmers rely upon horse power to plow their fields.

# NATIONAL CHARITIES AT WORK

Pets, wildlife, farm animals, and laboratory animals may all need help from charities. In every country, national charities do their best to help animals in danger, in addition to providing medical care. Many of these charities also offer free advice about how to best care for pets.

## The first animal welfare charity

In the United States, the ASPCA cares for all kinds of animals. It has branches, shelters, clinics, and centers throughout the country. Founded in 1866, the ASPCA employs a wide range of people, including animal welfare inspectors, veterinary workers, and animal-care assistants as well as fund-raisers, campaigners, and animal welfare scientists. There are groups similar to the ASPCA all around the world, some of which date back almost 200 years:

| Animal welfare charity | Year founded |
|---|---|
| The Royal Society for the Prevention of Cruelty to Animals (RSPCA), England and Wales | 1824 |
| The Ulster Society for Prevention of Cruelty to Animals (USPCA), Northern Ireland | 1836 |
| Scottish SPCA | 1839 |
| Sauver Protèger Aimer (La SPA), France | 1845 |
| The Ontario SPCA, Canada | 1873 |
| The New Zealand RSPCA | 1882 |
| The Humane Society of the United States (HSUS) | 1954 |
| SPCA Selangor, Malaysia | 1958 |
| RSPCA Australia | 1981 |

## The Humane Society of the United States

The Humane Society of the United States (HSUS) is another charity that tries to stop animal suffering and cruelty to animals. It is the largest animal protection organization in the country.

Throughout the United States, there are hundreds of independently run Humane Societies. These local organizations usually deal with providing shelter for animals, organizing adoptions, and educating the public. The national Humane Society does the same kind of work, but it is large enough to back big campaigns and recommend better laws for the welfare of animals.

## Follow the blog

Wayne Pacelle is the head of the HSUS. He contributes regular blogs to the society's web site. Subscribers to his blog can read and watch slide shows of the society in action. In June 2011, Wayne urged supporters to help save sharks by joining its campaign to stop the trade in shark fins. The same month, he backed the Take Your Dog to Work Day, promoted by Pet Sitters International.

### The Humane Society in action

On June 16, 2011, the breaking news on Wayne's blog was the rescue of nearly 300 dogs from a Puppy Mill (a dog-breeding center) in Hudson, North Carolina. It tells how the HSUS Animal Rescue Team helped the Caldwell County Animal Control (a local government-run organization providing animal care, rescue, education, and shelter) to rescue the animals from Mason Creek Kennel.

Adam Parascandola, director of animal cruelty investigations, went to the kennels. He described awful scenes of brutality and neglect. Mothers and puppies were kept in cramped wire cages. Many puppies could not move because their small paws had fallen through the gaps and gotten stuck. Some dogs had feces matted in their fur, rotting teeth, and infections. In other cages, rescuers discovered skeletons of dogs that had obviously been dead for some time.

The rescuers needed to wear masks to protect themselves from the harsh ammonia fumes caused by the buildup of urine and feces. Eventually, they were able to take all the surviving animals to an emergency shelter to receive urgent medical care.

# Cracking down on cruelty

Most people regard cats and dogs as "man's best friends." However, our furry friends are all too often the victims of cruelty. Organizations such as the ASPCA have a team of full-time inspectors responding to reports of cruelty and neglect seven days a week. Sometimes these inspectors need to take animals away from neglectful or cruel owners. Other times, they have to rescue an animal from a dangerous situation.

The inspectors save thousands of domestic, farm, and wild animals each year. Then, vets and other workers care for the animals in wildlife and animal rescue centers until they can be rehabilitated or found a new home.

## "Brave Heart"

One SPCA inspector working in South Africa earned himself the nickname "Brave Heart" after he helped to rescue a young Labrador dog from a hole in the earth 39 feet (12 meters) deep in Lyttelton, a suburb of Pretoria. The SPCA rescue team included three men: Hope Mokalapa, Shimmy Mashamaite, and Diale Ratsela. Hope Mokalapa managed to feed the animal for three days, while the team planned how to go about the tricky rescue operation. Action was delayed because the walls of the sinkhole were unstable and capable of collapsing at any time. Entering the sinkhole was dangerous: "We all played a part in rescuing the dog but going down the hole was a risk I was willing to take," said Shimmy Mashamaite, who eventually volunteered to go down the hole to rescue the dog.

"It took us about two hours to get the dog out with only one nylon rope and gloves," said Diale Ratsela. "If we had [had] better equipment it would have been much easier and safer. We decided to dub [call] Mashamaite 'Brave Heart' for his courageous act."

RSPCA officers rescue swans covered in oil. Jo Barr of the RSPCA says: "We don't know what the source of the oil is, but there has been some suggestion in the past it is boats illegally discharging fuel and oil."

### What it takes to be an inspector

It takes dedication and a genuine concern for animals to become an inspector for a group such as the ASPCA or for a state agency. Most inspector jobs have some requirements, some of which should ideally be linked with animals or science. Some groups also demand a farming or veterinary background, or at least previous experience working with animals. A love of animals goes without saying, but anyone wanting to join the profession needs to be able to cope with unpleasant situations. Inspectors have to deal with some terribly neglected or suffering animals, and sometimes they have to euthanize animals (put them "to sleep") to prevent further suffering. Inspectors also need excellent people skills, since they often have to deal with emotional or stressed owners. Anyone who wants to become an inspector has to undergo training and pass written exams.

## When disaster strikes

Natural disasters such as earthquakes, hurricanes, and floods are devastating to people and animals. Animal welfare charities all around the country respond during these emergency situations.

## Shelter in the storm

In August 2005, the deadly Hurricane Katrina struck the southern United States and broke through levees, the walls designed to hold back water during storms. New Orleans, Louisiana, and areas around the city suffered the brunt of the destruction, with huge loss of human and animal life.

The U.S. charity In Defense of Animals (IDA) is mostly known for its work campaigning for animal rights. Soon after the hurricane struck, the charity sent a rescue party to New Orleans. The situation was dire, with starving dogs being rescued from rooftops, cats being pulled out of the filthy water, and all kinds of pets saved from flooded homes. Six weeks later, the team had rescued nearly 1,000 animals.

In April 2011, rescue teams from several national charities were back in the South. This time, floods along the Mississippi River were threatening animals. The ASPCA worked together with PetSmart charities to provide help and shelter as well as treatment for many desperate creatures.

### Networking for animals

It is easy to keep up with the work of many animal welfare charities by going online. Numerous organizations, such as the ASPCA and Animal Welfare League, have joined social networking sites, including Facebook and Twitter. If you are old enough to join Facebook, you can find out what these charities are up to, see photographs of animals up for adoption, or simply show your support by clicking the "Like" button.

In the weeks following Hurricane Katrina, local charity groups and volunteers joined forces to rescue animals. These civilians are lifting stranded pet dogs to safety.

# The Tohoku disaster

In Japan, March 11, 2011, is a day that most people will never forget. A massive earthquake struck the country, causing a series of destructive tsunamis to sweep over the eastern coastline. Entire towns were washed away by the mighty waves. Thousands of people and animals lost their lives, and many more needed to be rescued.

There was more disaster to follow. The tsunami caused the meltdown of reactors in the Fukushima 1 nuclear power plant. Thousands of residents had to be evacuated from the area for fear of radiation poisoning. Some evacuees took their pets with them, but many had to leave their animals behind. The Tohoku disaster has been a terrible human tragedy, but animal welfare charities made sure not to forget the animals.

## Charities join forces

In times of crisis, charities often join forces to help. Japan Earthquake Animal Rescue and Support (JEARS) is formed of three Japanese animal welfare groups: Animal Friends Niigata, Japan Cat Network, and HEART-Tokushima pulled together to rescue animals lost or injured during the disaster.

## The challenge for rescuers

Isabella Gallaon-Aoki, who works with Animal Friends Niigata, visited the areas devastated by the tsunami. Many animals were dead, and those that survived needed urgent help. This was no easy task. Many roads were washed away, and there was a serious lack of gasoline for vehicles. Once rescued, the animals needed somewhere to stay. "I want to help the animals there and the owners who want their animals back... I wish there was more we could do," said Isabella.

## All aboard ARK!

The Japanese charity Animal Refuge Kansai (ARK) is doing its part to provide sanctuary for pets made homeless by the disaster. When the tsunami devastated large areas of land, the charity was ready for a large influx of animals and was set to create temporary shelters if numbers increased. ARK helped hundreds of animals within the areas evacuated around the Fukushima nuclear power plant.

Rescue workers entered parts of the zone to rescue pets that were tied up and starving. One woman asked ARK to rescue the cat she had left behind at her home, right next to the power station. This job was just too dangerous for ARK workers.

## To the rescue

ARK is determined to care for as many animals as possible that were affected by the disaster. It also aims to reunite as many animals with their owners as possible. The charity sends details and photos of the animals back to local authorities, to try to find their owners. In the meantime, providing free boarding and veterinary care costs a lot of money, and so the charity depends upon donations to do its work. ARK is also concerned about the animals still at large within the evacuation zone. It fears that within a year there will be a huge **feral** population of animals to contend with. By highlighting this problem, ARK hopes to get the Japanese government more involved in a rescue plan.

### ARK's rescue effort

As of May 29, 2011, ARK had rescued 197 dogs, 17 cats, a guinea pig, a rabbit, and a lovebird!

A Japanese victim of the earthquake and tsunami clings to her dog at an evacuation center in Kesennuma, north Japan.

## Education for the nation

National animal charities also play an important part in educating people about the basics of animal care. Many charities have web sites with useful information about caring for our pets, such as how to groom or feed animals. Some advice, such as opening the windows of a car on a hot day when there are dogs inside, is simple common sense. Even so, reports of animals dying from overheating in hot cars regularly appear in the news. This is why educating people remains at the heart of many animal charities' work.

## Ask the expert

The ASPCA in the United States has a web site full of tips for pet care, but users can also visit the "Ask the Expert" pages to find answers to their individual problems. Doctor Emily Weiss, the ASPCA senior director of shelter behavior programs, answers users' questions about horses on the web site. Horse owners have posted all kinds of questions, from "Why does my horse chew its feet?" to "Why has my horse suddenly become aggressive?" In the past, access to answers to these kinds of questions probably meant a trip to a vet. Now, people can receive the help they need to care for their animals with the click of a mouse!

Most animal welfare organizations believe education about animal welfare should start early. Web sites give tips about how to care for our pets. This includes information about their environment, diet, behavior, company, health, and welfare.

## Call of the wild!

National charities also keep people informed about how to care for wild animals. The Humane Society of the United States has a web site packed full of information about our "Wild Neighbors." Users can find out more about all kinds of wild animals living in their area, from bats and bears to raccoons and skunks. There are also plenty of tips for dealing with problems, particularly unwanted visitors such as snakes or opossums. In all cases, the HSUS advises people to remove the animals in the most humane way possible.

## Young people can help, too

RSPCA Australia is eager to encourage young people to care for animals. On its web site, young visitors are directed to the World of Animal Welfare (WOAW) pages. These pages are filled with fun things to do and learn about animals. Users can find out which animals have been brought into the RSPCA Wildlife Ward each week. They can read stories, such as the one about Gorilla the kookaburra, which flew into a car in New South Wales and became stuck in the front grille. After 17 days in the RSPCA hospital in Queensland, the little kookaburra was healed and ready to be released back into the wild. Like other animal welfare charities, RSPCA Australia also arranges educational visits to schools.

# WILDLIFE UNDERWATER

Animal welfare charities work hard on behalf of animals and creatures that live in the water. Many charities are busy helping animals such as seals, sharks, whales, dolphins, and sea turtles. Their work includes rescuing **marine mammals** trapped in nets or helping injured and sick animals.

There are also many conservation charities that aim to raise awareness of the threats these creatures face. These charities often work together with scientists who monitor the environment and research the animals. Armed with this information, the charities try to get the public involved by campaigning and fund-raising for the cause. This kind of work is very important because it helps to rescue individual animals and also to protect the future of entire species—some of which are endangered.

## Census of Marine Life

It is not only charities that act on behalf of marine animals. The Alfred P. Sloan Foundation is a **philanthropic** nonprofit organization. Established in 1934, the foundation supports and gives **grants** for research and education in science. A recent project to which the foundation has lent its support is the **Census** of Marine Life. This was a 10-year investigation of the diversity (range), distribution (numbers over an area), and abundance (quantity) of marine life. It was a massive undertaking, involving an international network of scientists and researchers from more than 80 nations. The results of the Census of Marine Life were released in 2010.

### The TOPP program

The Tagging of Pacific Predators (TOPP) research program was one of the many branches of research in the Census of Marine Life. It involved the **electronic tagging** of sharks to monitor their movements, and it allowed researchers to learn about their habits. This kind of information is very important for charities working with marine animals.

Marine charities suggest many ways in which individuals can help to protect marine life. If you eat fish, you should make sure that it is caught in a "dolphin friendly" way.

## Protecting the snubfin dolphin

In Australia, WWF supports the campaign to protect the snubfin dolphin. The species was only discovered in 2005, living in the northern waters of Australia. It is extremely rare and is endangered by the destruction of its natural habitat as well as the local fishing industry. Scientists do not know how many of these dolphins there are or much about them as a species. The lack of information makes it difficult to assess how to protect them. Together with the Northern Territory Government, WWF in Australia is trying to find out how many of the dolphins are being entangled in fishing nets and is working toward a better understanding of the species.

# A volunteer marine researcher's story

Global Vision International (GVI) works closely with international charities and other nonprofit organizations. Student Peter Robinson was eager to travel the world while doing something to help the environment. After exploring the opportunities available through GVI, he joined the GVI marine conservation expedition near Mahahual, in Mexico. This is Peter's account of his time spent on the project.

6 o'clock wasn't my usual waking hour, but waking up to a Caribbean sunrise every morning somehow made it worth it! After breakfast, my buddies and I put on our scuba tanks and climbed aboard the boats. Our task was to record the marine creatures we encountered and give approximate numbers. We noted whether they were swimming in groups or on their own. We also recorded what the animals were doing and whether this was normal behavior. These studies were conducted underwater and recorded on underwater slates [writing pads].

All this information contributed to GVI's ongoing work in the area to assess the condition of the coastline. Tourism in Mexico is growing, and so is the local town of Mahahual. Tourism poses a massive threat to the fish, stingrays, whales, dolphins, and other marine dwellers that live near the Quintana Roo Reserve, where our research camp was based. The information we collected will help people to understand how tourism endangers marine life. Hopefully, it will make them realize that the ocean needs protecting, and something needs to be done about it.

## Awesome animals

Back on the boats after our daily dives, we talked about all the awesome stuff we'd just seen. Neil saw a barracuda, Lucy saw a queen angelfish, and Jo and I were the first to see an African pompano— a tropical marine fish! The boat ride back was always full of excitement as we picked up speed and got sprayed by the waves. Once back on base we entered all our data, cleaned the boats, and filled the tanks full of air for the next dive. Then, after a generously prepared lunch, we'd get ready to do it all again. You couldn't help but wonder what you would see next time...a turtle, a whale, or even a shark? I was totally hooked!

## An unforgettable experience

Living on the beach for three months doing conservation work was a lot of fun—once you got over the lack of electricity and limited water for showers! The local community was extremely welcoming, and it was a great way to see a beautiful culture and contribute to protecting its natural environment. I'll never forget my time as a volunteer marine researcher. The experience has influenced what I'm going to do in the future. I've decided to devote my life and my career to conserving the environment.

### Helping hands

Each year, GVI sends more than 2,500 volunteers overseas to work on conservation and humanitarian projects (projects that help people).

A diver collects data about the coral off the island of Rongelap, Marshall Islands, Micronesia.

## Save the Whales

Another sea animal that unites many marine and environmental charities is the whale. The organization Save the Whales was founded by Maris Sidenstecker and her mother when Maris was just 14. Since 1977, the charity has aimed to educate the public—especially children—about marine mammals, their environment, and their preservation. The charity believes that the future of Earth and its animals lies in the hands of children, and that young people need to know that their actions have an impact on the environment.

Charities such as Save the Whales urge supporters to protest against live animal shows. This orca performs in a Sea World aquarium in Florida. Do you feel this is right? What do you think you could do about it?

### Whales on Wheels

One of Save the Whales' most successful initiatives is Whales on Wheels in California. These are educational presentations made with children in mind. During a typical workshop, children are able to touch skulls and skeletons of marine mammals or listen to whale and dolphin sounds. They also learn about how human actions on land have an impact on sea creatures. The message is that each person really can make a difference.

# The crocodile hunter

Crocodiles are not the most popular creatures on the planet. However, the Australian wildlife expert and conservationist, Steve Irwin, was passionate about them and earned himself the nickname "the crocodile hunter," although he never hunted the creatures to kill them! He found international fame hosting the wildlife program *The Crocodile Hunter*. Sometimes, his daredevil antics with animals such as crocodiles and snakes masked his dedication to animal conservation: "I consider myself a wildlife warrior," he once proclaimed. "My mission is to save the world's endangered species." Away from the TV cameras, Steve ran the Australia Zoo with his wife, Terri. In 2002, the couple set up the charity the Steve Irwin Conservation Foundation, which now goes by the name of Wildlife Warriors Worldwide.

## Wildlife hospital

Steve died in 2006, but his wife continues to run the zoo and its wildlife hospital. The hospital is located near Australia Zoo, at Beerwah in Queensland, Australia. It has an intensive-care room, laboratories, and enclosures for sick animals. The hospital employs a team of rescue workers, vets, nurses, and volunteers, who treat anything from Eastern water dragons to green sea turtles and platypuses.

Steve Irwin helped introduce many people to the fascinating world of wild animals. He also highlighted the vulnerability of many of these animals.

# Rescuing Nat

In June 2011, the "patient of the week" at Australia Zoo was Nat, a green sea turtle. The unlucky female turtle was beached onshore at Moreton Island, Queensland, when she was discovered by rescue workers. When Nat (as she was nicknamed) arrived at the hospital, resident vet Dr. Claude Lacasse made a full veterinary examination. She discovered that Nat was in considerable pain because she had swallowed one end of a fishing line, and the other end was wrapped around her front flipper. Nat was taken for X-rays, which revealed that the fishing line had worked its way down to the turtle's small intestines. The good news was there was no fishing hook attached. The bad news was that Nat needed an operation to remove the line. Nat was taken to the operating room, where Dr. Claude and a colleague performed the necessary surgery.

Nat was not out of trouble yet. The fishing line around her flipper had left a nasty wound and looked infected. Dr. Claude injected Nat with antibiotics. The turtle was then taken to dry-dock (an isolated tank filled with water to keep the animal comfortable) for 24 hours while she recovered from the surgery. Afterward, she was placed in the intensive care unit and was soon well on the way to recovery. In time, the team will be able to assess whether Nat is strong enough to be returned to the wild. However, if she requires full-time treatment, she may become a long-term resident of the zoo.

# Save the Seal Campaigns

When it comes to campaigning for animal welfare, the voices of many different charities and animal rights groups join together. One marine animal that has united many organizations is the seal. There are several kinds of seal, including gray seals, harp seals, and common seals. The plight of the harp seals in Canada is at the top of many anti-sealing groups' agendas.

The largest hunting ground for harp seals is in the Gulf of St. Lawrence in Newfoundland, Canada. Each year, about 4,000 fishermen use hakapiks (clubs) and guns to kill infant harp seals. The white fur from these baby animals is especially attractive and can be sold for large sums. Among others, the Canadian charity Harpseals.org is fighting to stop the slaughter of harp seals by hosting protests and outreach events. It encourages people to get involved by boycotting (not buying) Canadian seafood and writing to Canadian politicians and agencies to request a change in the law to stop the seal **cull**.

## Animal rights activities

Nonprofit animal rights organizations such as Sea Shepherd and People for the Ethical Treatment of Animals (PETA) are at the forefront of campaigns to stop the hunting of baby seals in Canada. Since 1976, Sea Shepherd has used **direct action** against the sealers. This has involved protesters **sabotaging** the hunters' attempts to kill the seals by getting in the way of the hunters or by removing the seals so they cannot be killed. Other times, the protesters have sprayed red dye on the baby animals to reduce the value of their fur. Activists have been arrested and imprisoned for their actions.

PETA is better known for its eye-catching publicity campaigns against cruelty to animals. In 2009, celebrities including Pamela Anderson and Kelly Osbourne gave their support and appeared in publicity shots for PETA's latest "Save the Seal" campaign.

Harp seals are most vulnerable for the short time they have baby white fur. Older seals are hunted for their oil and meat. These animals are also in decline due to pollution and being caught in fishing nets.

# SANCTUARIES AND SHELTERS

All around the world, there are individuals or small teams of people dedicated to animal welfare. Many of these people devote their lives to the creation of sanctuaries or shelters for a certain animal or group of animals, such as apes or reptiles.

## What are sanctuaries and shelters?

An animal sanctuary is a place where animals are cared for and looked after for the rest of their lives. An animal shelter is a place where animals are taken until they find a home or are rehabilitated into the wild. Animal charities usually offer one or both kinds of service.

## Small is beautiful

Many animal charities choose to concentrate their efforts on providing a place of safety for one kind of animal. For example, the Lone Pine Koala Sanctuary in Brisbane, Australia, provides care and sanctuary for koalas. In Tennessee, the American Eagle Foundation cares for injured and orphaned eagles and also supports projects to fully restore the bald eagle to the open skies.

### Spiderworld

A new charity called Spiderworld is on a mission to change the way people think about spiders. They say, "We love spiders and we want you to love them too!" At the end of 2011, the charity was little more than a "virtual sanctuary" for spiders. Visitors to the Spiderworld web site (www.wix.com/sadiemcbeth/spiderworld) can post questions about the creatures or find out more information about spiders in general. The charity hoped to set up a refuge for unwanted, confiscated, and mistreated spiders.

## Small-scale struggles

Rainbow Wildlife Rescue was founded by Birgit Sommer in Stephenville, Texas, in 2004. The nonprofit organization helps injured and orphaned animals such as raccoons, squirrels, opossums, skunks, and birds. After years of experience working with wild animals, Birgit strongly believes there is a need for human intervention to help wild animals. Birgit has rescued animals that have been shot, run over, poisoned, caught in traps, or even injured by lawn mowers.

Setting up her own rescue center has not been easy. Birgit has had to go through the lengthy process of applying for permits. She has juggled various online jobs so that she is able to stay at home to look after the animals. In 2011, she moved the rescue center to Weatherford, Texas, where she began rebuilding the wildlife enclosures. This is extremely expensive, and Birgit relies upon generous donations.

### Heartbreaking stories

Over the years, Birgit Sommer has helped many animals that have been injured or affected by humans. She says: "The stories and cases are endless and heartbreaking."

The naturalist and television host Steve Backshall (left, with animal expert Matthew Wright on a panel discussion in 2011) supports many animal charities. Steve is patron of the Exotic Pet Refuge. He also supports the Shark Trust, WWF, and many other groups.

# The Wildcat Sanctuary

The Wildcat Sanctuary (TWS) in Sandstone, Minnesota, is a safe haven for rescued wild cats. Big cats, such as tigers and lions, and small cats, such as cougars, bobcats, lynx, and serval, are cared for by a small team of employees and volunteers. The sanctuary was founded in 1999 by a young advertising executive named Tammy Thies. Tammy had her first taste of the "captive wildlife crisis" when she was involved in a photo shoot with a wild cat. Like many people, Tammy did not realize that wild cats were being used in this way. She then discovered that thousands of wild cats were being kept in appalling conditions at circuses and zoos throughout the country. She found out that many more wild cats were being kept as exotic pets. Tammy discovered that the trade in wild cats is big business, especially on the Internet.

The problem is that some states, such as Texas, have few laws regulating the keeping and breeding of exotic pets. In Texas, the breeding of tigers for trade is booming. Richard Farinato, an adviser with the Humane Society of the United States, believes that Texas probably has the largest population of tigers in the country.

## Tigers in Texas

*Some experts estimate there could be as many as 3,000 tigers in Texas, which means there are more tigers there than in the wilds of India!*

## The need for a safe haven

Caring for wild cats is difficult, so owners often set them free. U.S. news programs often carry stories about escaped wild cats—and, sometimes, they have attacked humans. Tammy was determined to set up a safe place for these abandoned animals.

## Expert care

TWS has become a sanctuary for more than 125 animals. They live in large enclosures, where they can roam freely and feel as close to nature as possible. TWS provides expert veterinary care for all its animals. However, sometimes TWS has to call in the specialists—especially if there is a big Bengal tiger that needs major dental treatment!

## Tiger teeth

Good dental care is a very important part of keeping wild cats healthy. Some animals have bad teeth because of a poor diet before coming to TWS. In May 2011, TWS welcomed a team of voluntary dental specialists from the Peter Emily International Veterinary Dental Foundation. Patients that day were Titan the Bengal tiger and Cody the cougar. Within four hours, four vets had completed four root canal treatments and six tooth extractions. The vets provided their services and use of equipment free of charge. It is this kind of generosity that keeps the sanctuary at the forefront of wild-cat welfare.

### Raising funds

As a nonprofit organization, TWS depends upon donations and fund-raising events. The sanctuary also has a hefty "wish list" with the web site Amazon. The list has everything from fire extinguishers to pooper-scoopers, food for the wild cats, and dental drills. Members of the public are invited to purchase items from the list to support the sanctuary.

The cheetah, also known as the "greyhound of cats" because of its speed, is in danger of extinction in parts of Africa. This sanctuary near Umfolozi, South Africa, houses rescued and sick animals.

## Behind the front line

There is much more to running any charity or animal sanctuary than attending to the needs of animals. There are many laws for setting up a charity or nonprofit organization, which vary from country to country. Once a charity has been established, there are administrative tasks that must be undertaken. All charities should operate professionally and follow certain rules. Larger charities employ teams of administrative workers to handle the large amount of paperwork that running a charity involves.

### Administrative jobs

A charity's administrative tasks include submitting annual reports (the yearly statement that provides the financial position of a company and the names of the officers and shareholders) and keeping track of the charity's accounts.

However, when individuals first set up a sanctuary or shelter, they may find it difficult to juggle paperwork with animal care. One example is the husband and wife team Roger and Fleur Musselle. They run Roger's Wildlife Rescue in Brighton, England. In a typical year, they care for more than 1,500 animals and birds in their home and garden. Roger and Fleur have not set themselves up as a charity because they would rather spend their time looking after animals than doing all the necessary paperwork required for running it. Instead, they rely upon donations and subscriptions to Roger's monthly newsletter.

## Mission accomplished

Many animal charities have been started because of the drive and dreams of one person or small group of individuals. The Born Free Foundation (see page 4) is a typical example of how one couple's mission developed into a worldwide organization.

## Studying orangutans

Dr. Biruté Mary Galdikas is another remarkable individual with a vision. She founded the nonprofit organization Orangutan Foundation International. Dr. Galdikas, a scientist, conservationist, and educator, is considered the world's foremost authority on the orangutan. She grew up in Canada and moved to the United States in 1964, where she studied psychology, zoology, and anthropology and developed her deep fascination with orangutans.

In 1971, Galdikas set up Camp Leakey in Tanjung Puting Reserve in Kalimantan, Indonesia, where she studied and worked closely with the orangutans. Galdikas's research was the first of its kind, and she is credited with bringing orangutans to the attention of people all around the world. In 1986, Dr. Galdikas, with the support of her colleagues, founded Orangutan Foundation International to support the important work for orangutans at Camp Leakey and around the world. The charity also cares for orangutans that have been in captivity and organizes their move back to the wild.

Elizabeth Svendsen founded the Donkey Sanctuary and its research center in 1969. The charity has helped over 14,500 donkeys.

# CARING FOR OLDER ANIMALS

Just as is the case with humans, the most vulnerable times in animals' lives are when they are born, when they are sick, and when they reach old age. Some animals have worked all their lives. Living and working conditions may not have always been good for them. Some charities understand the needs of retired and older animals. Sometimes they cannot provide that care, but they can help to find the care that is required.

## Anne waves goodbye to the circus

The story of Anne the elephant hit the headlines around the world in 2011. The elderly elephant (shown below) was believed to be about 57 years old. She had performed in the United Kingdom with the Bobby Roberts Super Circus since 1957. Between January and February 2011, the international campaigning group Animal Defenders International (ADI) secretly filmed Anne as she was beaten and kicked by her keepers, who were employed by the circus owners. Scenes of cruelty included Anne being whacked with a pitchfork, hit in the face, and kicked on her hind legs. (Anne had arthritis in her hind legs.)

Anne could not escape her beatings, since she was chained by the front leg. ADI sent this disturbing footage to the media. The public, campaign groups, and animal charities such as the Born Free Foundation began campaigning for her immediate release.

### Rescuing Anne

The owners of the Bobby Roberts Super Circus eventually handed Anne over to Specialist Wildlife Services. The keeper responsible for the cruelty to Anne disappeared overseas to escape arrest. Meanwhile, the Roberts family claimed they treated Anne as a pet and were upset about Anne's treatment at the hands of her keepers. However, after the film's release, the family was threatened, and circus attendance fell to an all-time low.

### Room to roam

In April 2011, Anne was rescued and taken to Longleat Safari Park in Wiltshire, England. She was given a home in a large, disused elephant enclosure where she could wander around freely. A team of veterinary workers reported that she was in fairly good condition. Fifty-seven years is quite old for an elephant, and she did not display any evidence of long-term beating. During her first week of freedom, she was watched over by a team of three keepers. They were pleased with her progress, noticing how playful and over-excited she sometimes became.

## Retired guide dogs

Guide dogs for the blind usually work until they are at least seven years old. What happens to these animals after a life devoted to guiding and helping a human being? Sometimes the family or individual who worked with the dog decides to keep it. In other cases, this is not possible, and the dog must find a new home.

There are plenty of shelters and sanctuaries that take in retired guide dogs and care for them until they find a new home. Shelter workers look out for extra-special new owners. Guide dogs have followed set routines and obeyed commands all their life. Adoptees should be able to help the dog adapt slowly to a new lifestyle. National nonprofit organizations, such as the Guide Dogs of America, have advice about how to go about adopting these special older animals.

# A sanctuary for elderly elephants

Luckily for Anne the elephant, she is getting all the care and veterinary attention she needs at Longleat Safari Park. But Anne's plight highlighted the need for an elephant sanctuary in the United Kingdom. The safari park has launched a campaign to build a sanctuary for elephants like Anne. The park is not a charity, but it does rely upon donations from the public to make the sanctuary possible.

The Elephant Sanctuary in Hohenwald, Tennessee, could be a blueprint for the new sanctuary. This nonprofit organization has been helping rescued elephants since it was founded in 1995. The sanctuary has taken in 24 elderly elephants, many of which have retired from the circus or zoos. With its lush green pastures, forests, ponds, and heated barns for cold winter nights, the sanctuary in Tennessee is the ideal place for elephants to retire.

## Bear care

Animal charities help elderly animals all around the world. In India, the charity Wildlife SOS has set up a number of bear rescue facilities, the most famous of which is the Agra Bear Rescue Facility in northern India. For hundreds of years, sloth bear cubs were snatched from their mothers by members of the Kalandar people. The Kalandars trained the bears to dance and entertain royalty.

In more recent times, the bears earned their keep by dancing for tourists. Not only did the cubs suffer the stress of being taken from their families, but they were also tethered to a rope for life. This was done by piercing their muzzles and passing the rope through the hole. Wildlife SOS set out to rescue every dancing bear. It did this by working with the Kalandars and providing them with incentives to surrender their animals.

## A rewarding day's work

Bear rescues took months of planning and persistent search and rescue attempts. By 2009, the charity had rescued what it believed were the last of the dancing bears. However, the sloth bear cubs are still **poached** for use in Chinese medicine, so Wildlife SOS continues to rescue them. As cofounder Kartick Satyanarayan says: "The feeling behind the arrival of each one of these bears is something that cannot be bought. At the end of the day all of us have the satisfaction of a rewarding day's work however hard it may be."

The owner of this sloth bear prepares to hand him over to the charity Wildlife SOS. The bear will spend the rest of its days at the Agra Bear Facility in India.

## A *helping hand for elderly animals*

There are hundreds of charities and nonprofit organizations caring for elderly or retired animals. Here are just a few examples:

• Asiatic black bears raised in Chinese factory farms for their bile can live out the rest of their days at Chengdu Moonbear Rescue Center, in China. This important work is supported by the charity Animals Asia Foundation.

• Rescued battery hens live as free-range chickens thanks to the UK nonprofit organization Little Hen Rescue.

• Primates retiring from scientific research or rescued from zoos and pet stores have a safe new home at the primate sanctuary Story Book Farm in Canada.

• Greyhound Angels Adoption finds new homes around New Jersey for greyhounds retired from racing.

# VOLUNTEERING

Most charity volunteers would agree that they get as much out of the experience as they put in. Knowing that you do your part to help animals, no matter how small, is a great feeling, and there are lots of ways that you can help.

## Put the "fun" into fund-raising!

Some fund-raising options are simple. You could get together with some friends and shake a collection can for your favorite charity at a local supermarket or shopping area. Charities want people to enjoy the fund-raising experience, so they also have some weird and wonderful ideas for raising cash. The truly adventurous can do a sponsored skydive or run a marathon.

## Dogs' dinners

ALIVE Rescue is an animal sanctuary in Chicago, Illinois. Its volunteers are always thinking up interesting fund-raising events, often with a doggy theme. Their fund-raisers include "Suds for Strays" (dog owners pay $10 to get their dog bathed by volunteers) and "Cooking for Canines" (dog owners learn how to cook up tasty treats for their pooches in return for a donation). These are great social occasions and raise money for ALIVE Rescue.

### A fund-raising recipe book

The Second Chance Animal Rescue Society (SCARS) in Athabasca, North Alberta, Canada, is a nonprofit organization with a mission to help unwanted pets such as dogs and cats. It relies upon the generosity of its supporters and fund-raisers. In 2010, the students from Landing Trail Intermediate School in Athabasca came up with a great fund-raising idea. The kids collected 400 recipes from their parents, teachers, and other students and created their own recipe book. They printed more than 300 books and sold them to family and friends. All together, they raised about $1,500 for SCARS.

## Hands-on help

If you are interested in working up close with animals, local charities are crying out for help. Dog and cat rescue charities often recruit volunteers to walk dogs, groom cats, help clean out cages, or assist with the day-to-day care of the animals. If possible, contact well-known charities such as your local ASPCA or Humane Society.

It is important to research these opportunities and talk with other volunteers before you commit yourself. Also, note that many charities only take volunteers who are 18 years of age or older, so that they can perform their duties unsupervised.

### Dog walking

If are not old enough to do an activity on your own, you could get an adult involved, too. Dog-walking for a dog rescue charity is an enjoyable activity that you could do with your family—and it is good exercise.

## Behind-the-scenes work

Remember, there are many other ways to help charities, such as doing administrative jobs in the office. You could help out in a charity store, which may involve anything from sorting the goods to helping behind the counter. Perhaps you could organize a collection of food and old blankets and towels for animal bedding and donate them to a local shelter.

The sky's the limit! Sponsored skydives and parachute jumps are a cool and effective way to make money for charity.

### Girl power

Freshfields Animal Rescue is a charity with animal sanctuaries in the United Kingdom. The organization aims to help unwanted, homeless, and abused animals. In Liverpool, England, the team cares for cats and dogs and more unusual pets such as chinchillas. The sanctuary in Wales is mostly home to horses and ponies. Among the volunteers at this sanctuary is 11-year-old Charlotte. She has spent her life around horses, so she feels confident working with the animals. Her day usually begins with feeding the ponies and horses. She then helps put the animals into different fields. Charlotte thinks she has gained a lot from her experiences:

"I have learned so much from the specialists that I have watched, like Andre the equine [horse] dentist, to the different problems that an animal can have... I have also learned that running a rescue center is very expensive and they are desperate for donations from people like you."

## Overseas opportunities

Voluntary charity work helps young people gain excellent work experience. Working with local charities may help you decide if a career working with animals is for you. Once you are over 18, you might decide to explore volunteer jobs overseas.

## Walk on the wild side

WWF Global has voluntary programs especially aimed at people between the ages of 20 and 27 years old who can pay for their own expenses. The global volunteer program needs young people to go to countries such as Madagascar, Fiji, and Peru. The application process is tough. Applicants must demonstrate their commitment to conservation. They must also have an ability to respect different cultures, take directions from supervisors, work well on a team, and have a thirst for ongoing learning.

## Enthusiasm for the job

International Animal Rescue (IAR) accepts volunteers of all backgrounds and nationalities. Professional volunteers such as vets or scientists are always in demand, but anyone who can demonstrate enthusiasm is welcome. IAR stresses that volunteering overseas is not always as glamorous or hands-on with the animals as many people think. Instead, many volunteers for IAR become involved in constructing rescue centers or other buildings.

### Trina's story

Some international volunteers are able to work with animals. Trina Sanderson, a veterinary volunteer in Romania, describes her work:

"This shelter has 800 dogs living here. Every dog is different and they each have their own unique story. It fascinated me and I fell in love with the place almost immediately... There are two [veterinary] doctors at the shelter. They are young but they are very skilled in what they do... The doctors are very patient with me and they want...me to learn. The shelter also receives calls to pick up injured or abandoned dogs and cats."

Workers from the Marine Mammal Research Center measure a turtle found on a beach in Mississippi.

# >> STATISTICS

## The problems

• The IUCN Red List of Threatened Species is the world's most comprehensive list of the conservation status of plant and animal species. In the 2011 Red List, it was stated that at least 1,134 mammals are believed to be threatened with extinction.

• The charity Polar Bears International publicizes information gathered by scientists around the world. It states that there are possibly 20,000 to 25,000 bears living in the wild, making the polar bear a threatened species.

• WWF states that wild tiger numbers have fallen by 95 percent in the past 100 years. In 2011, the number of tigers in the wild was estimated to be as few as 3,200. The South Chinese tiger, the Caspian tiger, the Javan tiger, and the Bali tiger are extinct in the wild. The future is bleak for all tigers, especially the Siberian, Sumatran, and Malayan tiger.

• Four million cats and dogs are put down in U.S. shelters each year—about one animal every eight seconds.

• The mighty mountain gorilla is critically endangered. In 2011, there were believed to be only around 720 to 740 of these animals left in the wild.

• The Humane Society of the United States estimates that there could be as many as 10,000 large wild cats in private ownership in the United States, many of which could be living in inadequate conditions.

## How charities are helping

• WWF reports that more than 1,000 new species were found on the island of New Guinea from 1998 to 2008. The list includes 218 new plants, 580 invertebrates, 43 reptiles, 134 amphibians, 2 birds, 71 fish, and 12 mammals. This shows that there are probably many more species of animals in the world that we do not know about!

• In the United States, the HSUS cared for more than 42,000 animals in 2010, and more than 8,300 animals were treated by vets.

• The charity SPANA helps working animals all around the world. Each year, 21 mobile clinics and 2 education buses travel about 447,000 miles (720,000 kilometers). That is the same as going to the Moon and back!

• In February 2011, Animal Defenders International rescued 25 circus lions from Bolivia. The rescue mission, called Operation Lion Ark, was coordinated by the organization following the ban on all performances involving animals.

• In seven years, Wildlife SOS India rescued more than 600 dancing bears. By December 2009, the charity believed it had rescued the last of the known dancing bears.

• The Global White Lion Trust spearheads a campaign to reintroduce the white lion back into the wild. The white lion was extinct in the wild, and as of 2006 there were 500 white lions in captivity. In 2006, four white lions were released back into the African wilds, and the reintroduction program continued successfully.

## Number of threatened species in 2011

This chart is an approximate illustration of the number of known threatened species—those that are critically endangered, endangered, or vulnerable.

VERTEBRATES

| | |
|---|---|
| Mammals | 1,134 |
| Birds | 1,240 |
| Reptiles | 664 |
| Amphibians | 1,910 |
| Fishes | 2,011 |

INVERTEBRATES

| | |
|---|---|
| Insects | 746 |
| Mollusks | 1,570 |
| Crustaceans | 596 |
| Corals | 235 |
| Arachnids | 19 |
| Velvet worms | 9 |
| Others | 24 |

# GLOSSARY

**campaign** planned activities intended to achieve a particular aim, such as a set of advertisements

**captivity** state of being imprisoned or confined in a small space

**census** usually, the count of the human population and a gathering of related statistics, undertaken by a government. The Census of Marine Life was conducted in a similar way to find out about life under the sea.

**climate change** long-term change in the patterns of weather experienced around the world

**confiscate** take something away from another person

**cull** slaughter of animals that reduces their numbers

**developed country** one of the richer countries of the world, including Australia and countries in North America and Europe

**direct action** activity to try to achieve a goal without using the normal political methods (for example, disrupting the activity of a group that is killing animals)

**documentary** movie, television program, or radio program that presents factual information about a political, social, or historical situation

**ecologist** person who studies the branch of biology that deals with the relations between living things and their environment

**electronic tagging** system used by scientists to monitor where animals are and the places they go to, by attaching a tag to them that logs such data

**enclosure** place for keeping animals that has a barrier or fence around it to stop them from escaping

**endangered species** species of animal that exists in such small numbers that it is in danger of dying out

**extinction** when a species has died out, or become extinct

**feral** used to be tame but is now wild

**global warming** increase in the average temperature of Earth's atmosphere and oceans

**grant** sum of money given to a person to use for a specific purpose, (for example, to help pay school fees)

**humane** acting with kindness or mercy

**marine life** plants and animals that live in the sea

**marine mammals** group of mammals that mostly lives in the sea or depends on the ocean for food. The group includes whales, dolphins, porpoises, manatees, dugong, some species of seal, walrus, and a few species of otter. Sometimes the polar bear is also called a marine mammal.

**microchipping** act of implanting a small microchip under the skin of an animal, so that it can be easily identified

**natural habitat** area or environment where an animal normally lives

**naturalist** expert or student of natural history (the scientific study of plants and animals)

**neuter** surgically remove a male animal's testicles so that it cannot father babies

**permit** document or certificate giving permission to do something, such as be allowed to own animals

**philanthropic** describes a person or organization that helps others, usually by donating money

**poach** catch and kill animals without permission on someone else's land

**primates** highest order of mammals, which includes humans, apes, and monkeys. Primates have hands, hand-like feet, a large brain, and forward-facing eyes.

**publicity** spreading the word about an issue—for example, through the media

**rehabilitation** process of preparing an animal for a return to the wild; this is done by treating sick animals and allowing them to practice survival skills

**sabotage** take action to ruin an activity you do not want to happen

**sanctuary** place where wild animals are protected

**sedate** make an animal go to sleep by giving it a sleeping drug

**spay** surgically remove a female animal's ovaries so that it cannot have babies

**tranquilize** use a drug to make an animal very calm

**vaccination** giving an injection to protect an animal against a certain disease

**welfare** health, happiness, and well-being

# ⟩⟩ FIND OUT MORE

## Books

Fischer, James. *The Power to Do Good: Money and Charity* (Junior Library of Money). Broomall, Pa.: Mason Crest, 2011.

Gay, Kathlyn. *Volunteering: The Ultimate Teen Guide* (It Happened to Me). Lanham, Md.: Scarecrow, 2007.

Gleason, Carrie. *Animal Rights Activist* (Get Involved!). New York: Crabtree, 2010.

Kaye, Cathryn Berger. *A Kid's Guide to Protecting and Caring for Animals* (How to Take Action). Minneapolis: Free Spirit, 2008.

Rochford, Deirdre. *Rights for Animals?* (Viewpoints). North Mankato, Minn.: Sea to Sea, 2006.

## Movies/documentaries

*Animal Nation: Our World, Their World* (Pegasus Entertainment, 2011)
Travel all around the world in these educational programs to discover more about the animals with whom we share the planet. Find out more about how humans are having an impact on the world's natural habitats and how this affects the lives of animals everywhere.

*Born Free* (see page 4), directed by Jack Couffer (Columbia Pictures, 2003; 1966)

*The Cove*, directed by Louie Psihoyos (Lion's Gate, 2009)

*Life* (see page 16), narrated by David Attenborough (Warner, 2010)

## Web sites

Animal Rescue Kansai (ARK): **www.arkbark.net/?q=en/node/1**
Learn about the Japanese organization that has helped after the tsunami there.

Anti-Cruelty Society: **www.anticruelty.org**
Find out more about the work of this animal charity.

ASPCA International: **www.aspca.org**
The ASPCA is a good starting point for people interested in the work of animal charities

Australia Zoo Wildlife Warriors: **www.wildlifewarriors.org.au**
This is the web site of Australia's largest wildlife hospital.

Born Free Foundation: **www.bornfreeusa.org**
Born Free is an international wildlife charity.

Elephant Sanctuary: **www.elephants.com**
Read about the sanctuary for elephants in Tennessee.

Humane Society: **www.humanesociety.org**
The Humane Society is another good place to begin research about the work of animal charities.

International Animal Rescue: **www.internationalanimalrescue.org**
Read case histories of rescued orangutans, dancing bears, and other wildlife all around the world.

Operation Baghdad Pups: **www.spcai.org/baghdad-pups.html**
Learn more about this program to keep soldiers and their war-zone pets together after the soldiers come back home.

Polar Bears International: **www.polarbearsinternational.org**
Find Information about polar bears and climate change.

Save the Manatee Club: **www.savethemanatee.org**
Learn more about the efforts of the Save the Manatee Club.

SPANA: **www.spana.org**
SPANA helps working animals around the world.

Wildlife SOS: **wildlifesos.org**
This group works to save the wildlife of India.

World Parrot Trust: **www.parrots.org**
Learn more about parrots and how to help to save them.

WWF: **www.worldwildlife.org**
WWF is the leading organization helping wildlife and endangered species in the world.

## Topics for further research

Research more about the following:
· the work of animal charities in your local area
· the effects of pollution on wildlife
· species at risk all over the world, and the reasons for their decline.

# INDEX